~A BINGO BOOK~

Educational
Books 'n' Bingo
EBB4886

Analogies Bingo Book: Primary Grades

COMPLETE BINGO GAME IN A BOOK

Written By Rebecca Stark

ISBN 978-0-87386-488-6

Educational Books 'n' Bingo

Printed in the U.S.A.

ANALOGIES: PRIMARY BINGO DIRECTIONS

INCLUDED:

List of Terms

Templates for Additional Terms and Clues

2 Clues per Term

30 Unique Bingo Cards

Markers

1. **Either cut apart the book or make copies of ALL the sheets. You might want to make an extra copy of the clue sheets to use for introduction and review. Keep the sheets in an envelope for easy reuse.**

2. Cut apart the call cards with terms and clues.

3. Pass out one bingo card per student. There are enough for a class of 30.

4. Pass out markers. You may cut apart the markers included in this book or use any other small items of your choice.

5. Decide whether or not you will require the entire card to be filled. Requiring the entire card to be filled provides a better review. However, if you have a short time to fill, you may prefer to have them do the just the border or some other format. Tell the class before you begin what is required.

6. There are 50 terms. Read the list before you begin. If there are any terms that have not been covered in class, you may want to read to the students the term and clues before you begin.

7. There is a blank space in the middle of each card. You can instruct the students to use it as a free space or you can write in answers to cover terms not included. Of course, in this case you would create your own clues. (Templates provided.)

8. Shuffle the cards and place them in a pile. Two or three clues are provided for each term. If you plan to play the game with the same group more than once, you might want to choose a different clue for each game. If not, you may choose to use more than one clue.

9. Be sure to keep the cards you have used for the present game in a separate pile. When a student calls, "Bingo," he or she will have to verify that the correct answers are on his or her card AND that the markers were placed in response to the proper questions. Pull out the cards that are on the student's card keeping them in the order they were used in the game. Read each clue as it was given and ask the student to identify the correct answer from his or her card.

10. If the student has the correct answers on the card AND has shown that they were marked in response to the *correct questions,* then that student is the winner and the game is over. If the student does not have the correct answers on the card OR he or she marked the answers in response to *the wrong questions,* then the game continues until there is a proper winner.

11. If you want to play again, reshuffle the cards and begin again.

Have fun!

VARIATION: You may want to ask students to give the correct answer after each clue. In that case, all the children will know what they are looking for on their boards.

TOPICS INCLUDED

bad	neck
big	noun
bird	ocean
boat	old
cow	out
day	pig
do	plural
dog	quick
don't	red
even	rich
female	sad
flower	see
four	smart
fun	smile
green	stop
hand	sun
he	tale
hear	talk
hot	three
immense	throw
kid	two
larger	under
leg	verb
liquid	walk
lose	write

EXAMPLE: big : little :: tall : short
This would be read "big is to little as tall is to short." For those just learning about analogies, you might want to write the clues on the board.

© Barbara M. Peller

Additional Terms

Choose as many additional terms/answers as you would like and write them in the squares. Repeat each as desired.
Cut out the squares and randomly distribute them to the class.
Instruct the students to place their square on the center space of their card.

Beginning Analogies Bingo

Clues for Additional Terms/Answers

Write two or three clues for each new term/answer.

_____	_____
1.	1.
2.	2.
3.	3.
_____	_____
1.	1.
2.	2.
3.	3.
_____	_____
1.	1.
2.	2.
3.	3.

A : a :: B : b	A : a :: B : b	A : a :: B : b	A : a :: B : b	A : a :: B : b
A : a :: B : b	A : a :: B : b	A : a :: B : b	A : a :: B : b	A : a :: B : b
A : a :: B : b	A : a :: B : b	A : a :: B : b	A : a :: B : b	A : a :: B : b
A : a :: B : b	A : a :: B : b	A : a :: B : b	A : a :: B : b	A : a :: B : b
A : a :: B : b	A : a :: B : b	A : a :: B : b	A : a :: B : b	A : a :: B : b
A : a :: B : b	A : a :: B : b	A : a :: B : b	A : a :: B : b	A : a :: B : b
A : a :: B : b	A : a :: B : b	A : a :: B : b	A : a :: B : b	A : a :: B : b

bad	big
high : low :: good : ___ good : better :: ___ : worse	little : mouse :: ___ : elephant large : ___ small :: tiny :: large
bird	**boat**
rose : flower :: canary : ___ ___ : parrot :: insect : bee	goat : ___ :: neat : seat water : ___ :: sky : airplane
cow	**day**
horse : colt :: ___ : calf ___ : moo :: cat : meow	minute : hour :: hour : ___ ___ : week :: month : year
do	**don't**
go : goes :: ___ : does ___ : did :: go : went	I've : I have :: ___ : do not ___ : contraction :: football : compound word
dog	**even**
cat : kitten :: puppy : ___ bark : ___ :: neigh : horse	north : south :: ___ : odd 8 : ___ :: 3 : odd

female

father : male :: mother : ___

mare : ___ :: stallion : male

flower

spaniel : dog :: tulip : ___

petal : ___ :: branch : tree

four

triangle : three :: square : ___

rectangle : ___ :: pentagon : five

fruit

salmon : fish :: apple : ___

___ : pear :: carrot : vegetable

fun

stop : mop :: run : ___

bun : ___ :: cup : pup

green

sky : blue :: grass : ___

___ : color :: chocolate : flavor

hand

sock : foot :: mitten : ___

arm : ___ :: leg : foot

he

she : her :: ___ : him

___ : singular :: they : plural

hear

go : going :: ___ : hearing

___ : heard :: do : did

hot

winter : cold :: summer : ___

warm : ___ :: cool : cold

immense small : tiny :: big : ___ tiny : ___ :: little : huge	**kid** sheep : lamb :: goat : ___ ___ : child :: grown-up : adult
larger big : bigger :: large : ___ ___ : largest :: better : best	**leg** elbow : arm :: knee : ___ ___ : foot :: arm : hand
liquid ice : solid :: water : ___ water : ___ :: steam : gas	**lose** open : close :: win : ___ ___ : lost :: play : played
neck glove : hand :: scarf : ___ necklace : ___ :: ring : finger	**noun** toss : verb :: ball : ___ girl : ___ :: walk : verb
ocean gift : present :: sea : ___ whale : ___ :: toucan : rainforest (Spell the word "sea.")	**old** high : low :: young : ___ new : ___ :: tall : short

out

up : down :: in : ___

___ : in :: above : below

pig

met : pet :: big : ___

___ : moo :: cat : meow

plural

book : singular :: books : ___

singular : ___ :: one : some

quick

slow : slowly :: ___ : quickly

___ : fast :: neat : tidy

rich

happy : sad :: ___ : poor

___ : wealthy :: pretty : beautiful

sad

sweet : sour :: happy : ___

___ : cry :: happy : smile

see

watch : watched :: ___ : saw

eye : ___ :: ear : hear

smart

clean : cleaner :: ___ :
smarter

___ : dumb :: dirty : clean

smile

healthy : ill :: ___ : frown

grin : ___ :: chuckle : laugh

stop

give : take :: ___ : go

red : ___ :: green : go

sun

Earth : planet :: ___ : star

___ : day :: moon : night

tale

see : sea :: tail : ___

___ : story :: fib : lie

talk

go : went :: ___ : talked

___ : speak :: answer : reply

three

square : four :: triangle : ___

triplets : ___ :: twins : two

throw

say : reply :: throw : ___

catch : ___ :: buy : sell

two

quartet : four :: couple : ___

___ : four :: four : eight

under

in : out :: over : ___

___ : below :: near : close

verb

ball : noun :: throw : ___

look : ___ :: mirror : noun

walk

run : ran :: ___ : walked

___ : walking :: read : reading

write

crayon : draw :: pen : ___

___ : wrote :: say : said

Beginning Analogies Bingo

© Barbara M. Peller

Beginning Analogies Bingo

kid	hot	larger	under	three
don't	big	two	ocean	immense
stop	rich		leg	plural
verb	bad	he	under	liquid
lose	walk	even	hand	hear

Beginning Analogies Bingo

Beginning Analogies Bingo

verb	tale	neck	red	lose
liquid	ocean	do	bad	smile
see	walk		female	he
green	smart	rich	out	immense
hear	two	even	don't	hand

Beginning Analogies Bingo

verb	he	ocean	under	stop
walk	big	cow	hot	old
bad	two		smile	bird
rich	see	lose	green	neck
hand	don't	even	out	larger

Beginning Analogies Bingo

rich	smile	lose	don't	larger
noun	do	hot	red	stop
leg	green		three	under
he	fun	two	even	cow
four	hear	quick	hand	plural

Beginning Analogies Bingo

hear	three	bad	do	don't
noun	he	cow	female	big
tale	plural		flower	larger
immense	smile	kid	out	four
ocean	even	sad	rich	leg

Beginning Analogies Bingo

bird	smile	neck	tale	plural
under	bad	four	hot	stop
red	cow		do	female
even	lose	out	quick	leg
liquid	he	kid	sad	larger

Beginning Analogies Bingo

kid	smile	sun	flower	ocean
liquid	larger	walk	big	noun
neck	under		female	boat
rich	green	stop	verb	see
even	don't	out	quick	bird

Beginning Analogies Bingo

leg	smile	day	under	boat
noun	tale	red	plural	do
stop	pig		larger	three
hand	rich	verb	four	green
two	even	quick	bad	liquid

Beginning Analogies Bingo

female	ocean	walk	stop	plural
four	tale	leg	bad	larger
old	kid		big	day
boat	hear	lose	flower	sun
green	out	cow	verb	three

Beginning Analogies Bingo

verb	under	do	red	sad
plural	boat	hot	big	larger
pig	smile		under	see
lose	immense	four	out	old
dog	liquid	neck	hear	leg

Beginning Analogies Bingo

bird	smile	bad	four	liquid
day	old	flower	female	hot
noun	tale		neck	walk
dog	stop	out	don't	verb
cow	even	kid	quick	ocean

© Barbara M. Peller

Beginning Analogies Bingo

ocean	three	old	under	female
walk	two	tale	quick	big
kid	sun		plural	red
even	green	larger	verb	noun
smile	day	pig	cow	boat

Beginning Analogies Bingo: Card No. 12

Beginning Analogies Bingo

dog	three	bird	old	plural
tale	day	smile	female	see
under	do		walk	sun
leg	out	boat	pig	verb
even	immense	quick	kid	flower

Beginning Analogies Bingo

don't	tale	bad	female	dog
boat	kid	old	big	smile
four	under		neck	cow
immense	out	pig	do	bird
even	red	see	liquid	leg

© **Barbara M. Peller**

Beginning Analogies Bingo

flower	female	bad	ocean	under
bird	neck	hot	tale	four
plural	kid		stop	larger
even	old	day	out	dog
liquid	green	quick	sad	walk

Beginning Analogies Bingo

do	old	day	sad	smart
red	see	sun	noun	under
dog	three		plural	walk
rich	boat	even	flower	verb
four	throw	quick	green	smile

Beginning Analogies Bingo

dog	talk	fun	old	don't
flower	four	out	under	sun
female	verb		throw	day
hear	liquid	leg	bad	see
lose	cow	ocean	under	three

Beginning Analogies Bingo

larger	pig	boat	four	red
smile	dog	lose	plural	cow
female	see		fun	sad
hear	hot	out	verb	neck
throw	old	bad	talk	bird

Beginning Analogies Bingo

plural	bird	old	day	pig
flower	under	sad	ocean	under
talk	don't		big	sad
neck	throw	lose	green	fun
stop	smart	liquid	leg	quick

© Barbara M. Peller

Beginning Analogies Bingo

pig	talk	under	old	big
do	walk	noun	lose	red
three	sun		rich	hot
hear	leg	hand	green	throw
he	two	smart	verb	fun

Beginning Analogies Bingo

flower	bird	noun	old	immense
three	fun	boat	day	kid
see	liquid		talk	bad
lose	ocean	throw	hear	leg
rich	smart	quick	dog	green

Beginning Analogies Bingo

stop	neck	fun	tale	dog
red	under	larger	day	big
boat	under		kid	sun
throw	hear	green	hot	don't
smart	cow	talk	see	noun

© Barbara M. Peller

Beginning Analogies Bingo

do	talk	ocean	tale	quick
bird	pig	liquid	flower	hot
neck	dog		hand	kid
see	smart	throw	cow	green
immense	leg	two	lose	fun

Beginning Analogies Bingo

do	pig	don't	talk	day
plural	quick	noun	red	kid
sun	sad		dog	see
immense	hand	throw	cow	three
he	rich	smart	under	two

Beginning Analogies Bingo

rich	noun	talk	bad	fun
hot	immense	flower	do	big
three	day		hand	throw
sad	hear	two	smart	under
quick	don't	boat	four	he

© **Barbara M. Peller**

Beginning Analogies Bingo

Beginning Analogies Bingo

fun	talk	hand	red	sad
lose	under	day	pig	do
immense	neck		under	rich
dog	tale	hear	smart	throw
sun	four	bad	two	he

Beginning Analogies Bingo

hand	boat	talk	pig	walk
immense	neck	flower	throw	big
out	two		smart	rich
sad	bird	noun	he	hot
dog	under	fun	stop	sun

Beginning Analogies Bingo

plural	pig	verb	talk	boat
walk	fun	hand	lose	under
two	see		sad	red
sun	stop	liquid	smart	throw
tale	female	dog	he	immense

Beginning Analogies Bingo

fun	pig	sad	flower	female
immense	lose	noun	sun	stop
three	hand		big	talk
walk	hear	larger	smart	throw
do	day	he	bird	two

© **Barbara M. Peller**

Beginning Analogies Bingo

don't	talk	red	female	throw
hot	sad	neck	under	big
he	cow		sun	noun
immense	bird	pig	smart	hand
hear	ocean	two	fun	larger

www.ingramcontent.com/pod-product-compliance
Lightning Source LLC
LaVergne TN
LVHW061336060426
835511LV00014B/1957